Begin 21

Your First 21 Steps with Jesus

Timothy Eldred

BroadStreet
PUBLISHING

ENDEAVOR
RESOURCES

BroadStreet Publishing Group, LLC
Racine, Wisconsin, USA
BroadStreetPublishing.com

Begin 21: Your First 21 Steps with Jesus

Copyright © 2016 by Timothy Eldred

ISBN-13: 978-1-4245-5426-3 (softcover)
ISBN-13: 978-1-4245-5437-9 (e-book)

Stock or custom editions of BroadStreet Publishing titles may be purchased in bulk for educational, business, ministry, fund-raising, or sales promotional use. For information, please e-mail info@broadstreetpublishing.com.

Art direction by Kelton Eldred
Cover by Chris Garborg at GarborgDesign.com
Interior by Katherine Lloyd at theDESKonline.com

Printed in the United States of America
16 17 18 19 20 5 4 3 2 1

Contents

Week 3 – Voice • 67

Foreword

My name is Benny Proffitt. From my childhood, I believed in God. I went to church with my family and tried to be a good person, so I thought everything was okay. Then, one day in my adolescence, someone challenged me with the most important question I was ever asked: "What will you do with Jesus?"

The complexity of that question went far deeper than, "Do you believe in Jesus?" Many can say yes to that question because most people do know *about* him; they believe he was a real person who lived here on earth. Some even consider him to be one of the greatest teachers or philosophers of all time. Others go as far as to say that he was a godly man. But while all of these statements are correct, they don't even scratch the surface of who Jesus is.

To answer "What will you do with Jesus?" requires deeper contemplation. It means we must consider that he came to earth to fix things. His purpose was to restore our relationship with God—through showing us how God wants us to live and by paying the penalty for our selfish choices by dying on a cross because he loves us so much. He alone is the way to experience the life that God intended, and he's the only path to eternal life.

One of the most famous verses in the Bible sums up God's plan and the life of Jesus this way: "For God so loved the world, that he gave his only Son, that whoever believes in him should not perish but have eternal life" (John 3:16).

Answering the question of "What will you do with Jesus?" begins with believing that the claims about him in the Bible are completely true—that without him life is meaningless, yet with him we can know God's plan and purpose for today and have hope for tomorrow.

I answered this question for myself over fifty-five years ago as a young man and gave my life to Jesus. That's when everything started to change. Over the years, he has filled me with love, joy, and peace. He actually lives within me. Time and time again he has proven to me that I can fully trust him with everything. I have assurance of who I am because Jesus rescued me.

So, as you can see, I am not ashamed to call him my Lord and Savior.

Chances are, you're reading this book because you've either recently given your life to Jesus or you're considering the question. If you've decided to make him the master of your life, this book will help you understand your next steps. If you're still contemplating becoming a Christian, I encourage you to walk through the twenty-one days with an open mind to learn more about what following Jesus means. As you read, he'll make himself known to you.

Accepting Jesus isn't complicated. It begins by admitting that you need a new start that only he can provide, which is as easy as saying a simple prayer like this:

> Dear God, I believe that Jesus Christ is your Son. You sent him to show the world a better way. I believe that he died on a cross to save me from sin. His death paid for my mistakes, and his resurrection from the dead gives me eternal life. I confess that I can't live without him. My life is not my own anymore. I give it to you and accept Jesus as my Lord and Savior. In his name, amen.

If you said that prayer, the Bible says you've become a brand-new person. You've taken the first step into God's plan and purpose for your life. Now it's time to discover what it means to be a follower of Jesus. Just take one day at a time and trust him to change your world completely.

Benny Proffitt
Founder of First Priority
Executive Producer, *I'm Not Ashamed*

Introduction

You've just taken a big step. Huge. Gigantic. Massive actually. And that can't be overstated. Saying yes to Jesus Christ will be the greatest decision of your life. But your choice wasn't an accident. It wasn't a fluke, and it certainly wasn't a coincidence. It was *planned*.

So were you.

God chose you even before you chose him. From the beginning of time, his plan included you. God had you in mind. He handpicked you. On purpose.

Then when you said yes to God's offer to receive Christ, he responded freely. He welcomed you into his family. Arms wide open. He now looks at you and says, "That one is mine." He's given you a handwritten invitation, and you've accepted it. Now you're a child of the one true God. Nothing can ever change your new status.

What did you do to earn this? Nothing. Nada. It was a gift. Jesus paid for it—with his own blood. It cost him everything to secure your salvation, and he has given you a new life. So you can stop worrying about looking backward. Your past? Behind you. Your mistakes? Erased. Your future? Secure. Eternity? Bonus!

Now it's time for you to step forward into your part of God's plan. I'm sure you have questions: How do I do that? What about tomorrow? How does this Jesus thing work? What's my next move?

Those are great questions. And you'll have a lot more as you grow as a Christian. But don't worry. God didn't put you on his team to let you fail. He won't drop you. Or let you bomb.

Don't let naivety trip you up though. Some days will be harder than others. Exhausting. Even discouraging. There's no shallow end of the Jesus pool. You don't get time to wade in or warm up; you're in deep water right away.

So what should you do first? Simple. Find a mentor. Attach yourself to someone with more experience—a swimming buddy of sorts—who's been following Jesus for quite some time. Age doesn't matter. Just choose someone who isn't a newbie.

Your mentor doesn't need to do everything right. Nobody does. But they can certainly teach you the basics, as well as help you stay afloat. They'll provide you with necessary help: encouragement, accountability, support, and, perhaps most importantly, friendship.

Watch them closely. Learn from their life. Follow their example. Hang onto them tightly if needed. Squeeze hard. Before long, someone will be holding onto you as *their* mentor, and you'll be sharing what you've learned about following Jesus.

Companions like this are crucial in the Christian walk. There's safety in numbers. We help each other and watch each other's back. But the real power to remain faithful, following Jesus for a lifetime, comes from him. You have his Spirit, so trust him for your strength. He actually lives *in* you now—and he'll live *through* you too.

The next twenty-one days will be very important for you to understand what you've jumped into with Jesus. To help you along, we're giving you a simple plan to get your new life started. It won't answer all of your questions—that will take time—but it'll point you in the right direction.

Think of each day as a step, not a leap. Small but significant. Every page of *Begin21* contains basic ideas that will help you:

• Develop your relationship with Jesus

- Live out your new identity in Christ
- Find your voice in God's story

So hang on. Hold nothing back. This is going to be a thrill ride. Make Jesus your best friend. Your number one. Your rock. And he'll transform your world.

For Mentors to Read

Too often, new followers of Jesus flounder. Some even fail. They hear God's call, accept his invitation to follow Christ, and dive right into the deep end of the Jesus pool without knowing how to swim.

They can feel alone. Overwhelmed.

In time, they tire and can barely keep treading water. Many begin to sink in a slow descent to the bottom. Desperate. Disillusioned. Spiritually dying. All before they begin to really experience the exhilaration of this new life.

It's a sad reality, but a preventable tragedy.

That's where you come in. Your role is vital. As a mentor of a new Christian, you're important to the first steps of their spiritual journey.

Begin21 provides a path for helping new believers develop their relationship with Jesus, live out their new identity in Christ, and find their voice in God's story. Think of it like freshman orientation.

Your new protégé needs a steady partner. A stroke-by-stroke companion. You can be the life guard and coach that prevents them from needing spiritual life support. That's your assignment.

They trust you. Because they chose you. On purpose.

Over the next twenty-one days, you'll help them learn. Answer questions. Explain steps. Take steps with them. Show them how it's done. And watch them do it on their own. It's a powerful process.

Be involved as much as needed and no more. Don't do anything *for* them—only *with* them. Your guidance will give them confidence and affirm their progress. As they learn from your example what it means to love God with everything they've got, you'll see a new life in Christ emerge before your eyes.

Be purposeful over the next three weeks. Give this assignment the time and attention it deserves. God's power, your praise, and the new principles your mentee will learn are a winning combination. A proven recipe for a fresh start with a great beginning, middle, and end.

Now, sit down together and make a three-week plan for how you're going to proceed. Then trust Jesus to do the rest. He'll show up and show off. And you'll get to share in his joy!

Week 1

RELATIONSHIPS

Lives are changed through relationships, and relationships that change lives take time. It's all about relationships. From the beginning of human existence, God made it clear that we were created for community with him. And with each other.

The Creator already knows you. He does. Inside and out. And he loves you for who you are. There's no need for playing games. No pretending. You don't need to fake anything with your heavenly Father. You can be yourself. Even on your worst days, God sees the best in you because he sees you through Jesus. When you try your best and fail, you're still loved and still forgiven.

God wants you to know him too. He wants you to hear his heart, feel his love, learn his ways, and draw from his strength. On the good days and the difficult ones—every day and any day—he will never let you down.

But having a deep relationship with God doesn't

just happen. It takes real effort on your part. Getting to know God personally must be a priority. Jesus showed us how it works, so we'll learn from him in the next few days. We'll follow his example.

We also need relationships with others who follow Jesus. Having a mentor is a great way to start, but it's only the beginning. There's a much larger Christian community out there called the church. You need them, and they need you (more on that later).

So we're going to look at building our relationship with God and with others this week. Let's start by thinking about what you already know about relationships. You're closer to some people than you are to others. You feel safe and secure around certain individuals whom you consider close. More than likely, the people you know and trust best are those you spend time with most.

That's the key to healthy relationships. *Time.* It's a precious gift—but it's limited. So it has to be used well. Invested. Not just spent. There's a difference. Making an investment means putting something aside now to gain something better later. But here's the twist: When you spend time with Jesus, you're not giving up anything. You're investing. So you're gaining. Growing. Becoming.

As you get to know him more, he'll make changes in your life. But you won't be losing out. You'll just be learning to let go and make room for something new. God will fill those empty spaces in your life with something bigger and better: more of Jesus. He's your friend. Hero. Savior. Get to know him. Soon you'll see that you lack for nothing.

You're complete in Christ.

Spend Time with Jesus

"If you look for me wholeheartedly, you will find me."
Jeremiah 29:13 NLT

The Bible is God's word. It's a guidebook—an instruction manual—and every statement in it is true. God can't lie. Ever. No, really. You can trust that he'll always do what he says.

This Bible verse from Jeremiah is an IFTTT (if-this-then-that) statement. It's both a principle and a promise, and it's one of the most important guidelines you can learn as you begin your Christian walk.

Did you know that Jesus himself practiced this IFTTT rule? Here's just one example: "But Jesus often withdrew to the wilderness for prayer" (Luke 5:16 NLT).

Jesus' example teaches us that it's hard to have

a good conversation in a crowd, whether you're on a busy street, in a noisy classroom, or any place where you can't concentrate. You can't hear what people are saying, and they can't hear you either. Most meaningful talks take place one-on-one in a quiet place, and they're quite often planned. Intentional. They don't just happen by accident.

The Christian life isn't a religion. It's a personal relationship with the Savior of the world. The more you get to know Jesus, the more you gain. You'll find peace, strength, comfort, and joy.

So set daily reminders. Schedule time to spend alone with Jesus—just the two of you in a quiet place getting to know each other. Talk to him. About everything. Honestly. And listen. You'll learn to recognize the sound of his voice.

And no. Jesus will never stand you up. He will never betray you or break your heart. This is a safe relationship.

Question ?

What causes us to hold back and be less than open and honest with people?

Challenge ❗

You can be honest with Jesus. Ask God to show up as you spend time looking for him. Notice the places you see him and the times he reveals himself to you.

(Thoughts)

Write down anything on your mind from day one. Talk openly and honestly with your mentor about these questions and comments.

Start Praying

Once Jesus was in a certain place praying. As he finished, one of his disciples came to him and said, "Lord, teach us to pray, just as John taught his disciples."

Luke 11:1 NLT

Jesus had students—and like you, they were handpicked. He saw their potential, so he invited them into his plan. Then he spent three and a half years training them in God's ways.

But even though Jesus often withdrew from his protégés to pray alone, his destination wasn't a secret. His pupils knew the purpose of his privacy. They knew the power of prayer, so they said, "Show us how it's really done."

Like all good teachers, Jesus modeled everything he taught. He passed on truths, tricks, and techniques. He didn't hide his know-how. When his interns probed about prayer, he boiled it down to the basics for them:

"Our Father, dwelling in the heavenly realms, may the glory of your name be the center on which our lives turn. Manifest your kingdom realm, and cause your every purpose to be fulfilled on earth, just as it is fulfilled in heaven. Give us today the bread of tomorrow. Forgive us the wrongs we have done as we ourselves release forgiveness to those who have wronged us. Rescue us every time we face tribulation and set us free from evil. For you are the King who rules with power and glory forever. Amen" (Matthew 6:9–13 TPT).

There are many ways to pray. Jesus could have lectured on every variation, but he didn't. Instead, he made it simple.

You don't have to complicate it either. Just add prayer to your time with Jesus. Pray aloud or silently. Pray while sitting, standing, or watching Netflix. There's no right or wrong way. Just begin with "Dear God" and end with "in Jesus' name, amen." The words in the middle are how you express your heart. Let them flow, and then take time to listen.

Question ❓

What have the prayers you've experienced before now been like?

Challenge ❗

If prayer is a form of conversation with God, what could he be saying to you? When you talk to him in prayer, take time to listen. Share what you're hearing with your mentor.

Thoughts

Write down anything on your mind from day two. Talk openly and honestly with your mentor about these questions and comments.

Read the Bible

> Every Scripture has been written by the Holy Spirit, the breath of God. It will empower you by its instruction and correction, giving you the strength to take the right direction and lead you deeper into the path of godliness. Then you will be God's servant, fully mature and perfectly prepared to fulfill any assignment God gives you.
>
> *2 Timothy 3:16–17 TPT*

Everyone loves a good story. It's fun to hear, easy to remember, and simple to share. The Bible is a good story—God's story—and it's true, not a fairy tale. It's God's words in print for us to read, remember, and retell. Generation after generation.

Some people think the Bible is just a bunch of rules—a book of *don'ts*, *can'ts*, and *shouldn'ts*. They believe it's God's way of keeping them from having fun or that it's boring. But that's wrong. Nothing could be further from the truth. The Bible has action. Love. Blood. Mystery. Risks. It also keeps us safe, protecting us and saving us from suffering the consequences of poor decisions.

As we read about all the people in God's story, we learn from their lives. We see their ups and downs, their fears and victories. And throughout the Bible we see how God shows his love for the world over and over again.

But how do you read it? Where do you begin?

Since you're just entering the Christian life, it's best to start reading about Jesus. The first four books of the New Testament (the second part of the Bible) are called the Gospels. These books are a great place to learn about his life and teachings. Start in the book of Matthew by reading chapters 5 through 7 (they're pretty short). These chapters are Jesus' first speech to a large crowd where he flips their understanding of God upside down.

Reading the Bible is like praying. You get the same outcome, since you're hearing God's voice and connecting to his heart. It's relationship building— another way he created for us to get to know him.

Add Bible reading to your time with Jesus. Get a copy of your own, or download one at Bible.com.

Question ❓

Where does your view of the Bible come from? What questions do you have about the Bible that you would like to have answered?

Challenge ❗

Read from the Bible today. As you begin to explore what the Bible says, find a safe place to ask questions that build your trust that God's story is 100 percent true.

(Thoughts)

Write down anything on your mind from day three. Talk openly and honestly with your mentor about these questions and comments.

Make New Friends

"A new commandment I give to you, that you love one another: just as I have loved you, you also are to love one another. By this all people will know that you are my disciples, if you have love for one another."

John 13:34–35

Have you ever moved into a new place, or do you know someone who has? It can be hard. You stick out even though you try to fit in, and it doesn't always work out as you'd hoped.

Jesus knew what it was like to be the outsider—to feel alone, left out, and isolated. He also knew his followers would have this same experience, so he created a "club" called the church and told all the members to basically "Stick together. In love."

Some people think the church is just a building or maybe a weekend event. But it's so much more than that! The church is people; it's the group name Jesus' gave his followers. When you accepted Christ, you became a member of this special group of faith-filled friends.

Since you're new to the Jesus thing, you might not know too many church people. But you need to. Your mentor is a member and should be able to help you get connected.

Why is this so important? Because we need each other. Alone we are weak and vulnerable, without protection. We're stronger together, like a team. Each person does their part and plays their position. Together we help one another grow into the people God intended.

The church comes in all shapes and sizes. Some people meet in large groups in buildings. Others meet in small groups in homes. On campuses, in basements, in dorms, or even coffee shops. The church is everywhere, so find a group you like and make Christian friends.

This community of Jesus followers can be your support system. And as other people notice your love for each other, you'll be able to tell them about Jesus.

Question ?

Who are the groups of Christians you know that show they are Jesus' followers through a lifestyle of love?

Challenge !

Take steps to lock arms with a Christian group to get the support and friendship you need.

°
o
(Thoughts)

Write down anything on your mind from day four. Talk openly and honestly with your mentor about these questions and comments.

Day 5

Tell Your Story

But in your hearts revere Christ as Lord. Always be prepared to give an answer to everyone who asks you to give the reason for the hope that you have. But do this with gentleness and respect, keeping a clear conscience, so that those who speak maliciously against your good behavior in Christ may be ashamed of their slander.

1 Peter 3:15–16 NIV

"Are those new shoes?"

"Did you get your hair cut?"

"When did you start wearing glasses?"

"Is that a new piercing?"

We notice when there's something different about a person. Sometimes it's physical, while other times it's behavioral or emotional. Often, we ask them about the change, especially when it's obvious.

As you build your relationship with Jesus, he's going to make a difference in you. You're going to

31

become more like him. You'll see the world differently, viewing people in a new way and living with a fresh perspective and attitude about life. And people will notice.

Jesus won't alter everything about you though. The qualities that make you unique—for example, your talents, abilities, and strengths—won't change. But he'll teach you how to apply them in new ways.

Instead of being self-focused like much of the world, you'll begin to see others as more important. Your compassion will grow, and your kindness will show. God's love will lead your lifestyle.

Not everything will be evident … at least not at first. Transformation takes time. But don't be shocked when people ask, "What's different about you? Has something changed?"

Be ready to speak up for Jesus. Talk him up. You don't need to know everything about him to be able to tell others what he's done in your life. Just tell your story. And smile. No one can argue with that.

Question ❓

Have you already noticed differences in your life since you accepted Jesus? Are there other areas you'd like him to change?

Challenge !

Make a list of other areas of your life you'd like Jesus to change. Share them with your mentor.

Thoughts

Write down anything on your mind from day five. Talk openly and honestly with your mentor about these questions and comments.

Say Thank You

Give thanks in all circumstances; for this is the will of God in Christ Jesus for you.

1 Thessalonians 5:18

Have you ever felt used or been taken advantage of by someone? Has there been someone who seemed to want something from you but would never offer anything in return? Not even a thank-you? It's like you're a juice box—sucked dry until there's nothing left, not even air. You feel flat and empty.

That's no way to build a healthy relationship with anyone. Even if you like giving to others, it's nice to be thanked at least every once in a while. A little gratitude really does go a long way. It makes us feel appreciated and lets us know that our friendship matters.

Relationships require give and take. They can't be one-sided. Always taking and never giving. This is true of our relationship with God as well. But what can we possible offer the Creator of the world?

Well, not much. Giving God a gift is like trying to buy a present for the person who owns everything. It's impossible. So how can we show our appreciation for Jesus and for the new life we now have in him? The answer is simple: we can offer our gratitude, thanks, and praise.

We spend a lot of time asking God for things when we pray. (He's happy to listen, so don't stop. He'll always do what's best for you, even if he says no.) But our conversations with him should also include recognition. We must be grateful—not because it's a rule, but because he deserves our appreciation.

Grateful people are happier. They find good in everything, and it shows in their life. So give God thanks no matter what you're facing. Your relationship with Jesus will be stronger. And so will you.

Question ?

What things in life keep gratefulness out of your reach?

Challenge !

*Examine your life for a few things you are grateful for,
then make them the focus of your prayer time today.*

Thoughts

*Write down anything on your mind from day six. Talk
openly and honestly with your mentor about these
questions and comments.*

Take a Load Off

> And on the seventh day God finished his work that he had done, and he rested on the seventh day from all his work that he had done. So God blessed the seventh day and made it holy, because on it God rested from all his work that he had done in creation.
>
> —*Genesis 2:2–3*

o I have to do everything around here?"

Have you ever heard someone make that statement? Or maybe you've said it yourself? These are the words of a person who's tired. Worn out. Frustrated.

If we're not careful, we can push too hard. Hit a wall. Crash. And that's not healthy. Even God took a break once creation was complete. But we don't just need a nap or a good night's sleep. We need a real rest—a time when we unplug from our crazy lives to recover.

Does that mean we push pause on Jesus? Not at all. It means we push *into* Jesus. We rely on him and trust that he'll complete his work even while we rest in him. He's the Savior of the world. He'll finish God's plan, complete the project, and pull off the impossible.

Following Jesus includes trusting God enough to take a load off—one day once a week. We use this time to reflect, and we can slow down without worry because God doesn't. He's always at work transforming our world. Inside and out. And he invites us to join him in his work:

"Simply join your life with mine. Learn my ways and you'll discover that I'm gentle, humble, easy to please. You will find refreshment and rest in me. For all that I require of you will be pleasant and easy to bear" (Matthew 11:29–30 TPT).

Rest is required for a healthy relationship with Christ. Lean on him. Feel his heartbeat. He's Gatorade for the soul. As you rest in him, you'll discover your true identity as one of God's chosen children.

Question ❓

Think of someone you trust. How do you feel when you're around them?

Challenge ❗

Take some time to think about the connection between trust and rest. Practice resting, and know that God is in control and cares deeply for you.

Thoughts

Write down anything on your mind from day seven. Talk openly and honestly with your mentor about these questions and comments.

Week 2

IDENTITY

ason Bourne. Maybe you know the name. He's a character in a series of movies about a government agent suffering from amnesia and trying to figure out exactly who he is. Except for the secret spy stuff, his journey is not much different from our own. We're all looking for identity.

Each of us wants to be somebody. We want to matter. Deep down we seek significance. We crave authenticity, not artificial flavoring. The planet is already filled with phony people. Posers. Pretenders. It's no wonder why there's so much pain in our lives.

How would our world change if we understood our true identity as God's handpicked? What would be different about our social media posts? Our opinions of others? Even how we see ourselves?

Our behavior is based around our sense of identity. So like Bourne, we search. No matter the cost or risk. Discovering our true self is the key to becoming the person God intended, and we all want to be genuine. The real deal.

Last week you focused on building a relationship with God through your new faith in Jesus. You learned action steps to produce intimate interaction with your Creator. Each day was designed to lay a firm foundation with him. Something solid to stand upon. A secure footing.

Identity is born out of intimacy. It's the result of relationships, and as you continue to engage with God, he will reveal the real you. So drill down. Go deeper. Depend on him daily to discover your identity.

Your adoption into God's family through Jesus gave you a position. No more wondering about your place in the world. You're an overcomer. A leader. A servant. A messenger of hope. These are just of few of your birthmarks—and birthrights—because you belong.

Too many people spend their whole life trying to invent their importance. Instead of embracing their belonging, they're busy trying to blend into the crowd. That doesn't have to be you. Never again.

The goal this week is to help you live out your new identity. There's no need for spiritual amnesia.

Your relationship with God is solid. But in case your memory starts to get foggy, these practices will help you remember who you are.

Hopefully you're getting a little more comfortable in the deep end of the pool. The shock you might have experienced at first is being replaced by peace. You're becoming more comfortable—and buoyant. As you listen to God this week, he'll continue to build your confidence. You'll begin to understand your identity, how to love yourself, and how to treat others who are covering up their fears by being fake.

When you know who you are in Christ, it becomes clear how to let Jesus live through you. But it doesn't happen overnight, so don't get anxious. This is a marathon, not a sprint.

Think Ahead

"For I know the plans I have for you, declares the LORD, plans for welfare and not for evil, to give you a future and a hope. Then you will call upon me and come and pray to me, and I will hear you."

Jeremiah 29:11–12

When we fail to plan, we plan to fail.

Read that again. Out loud. It's not a new idea. Lots of people have said it for many years, especially successful people, which is probably why we should pay attention to it.

Last week we talked about the importance of time. We said it was a gift—but limited. Sometimes if we're not paying close attention, we run out of minutes and miss due dates. We get busy in the moment and fail to hand in homework. Or we forget to put on deodorant. So we must learn to think ahead.

God is always thinking ahead for us. His plans include our future. It's called heaven. When he says, "Time's up," we still have hope. We were made to live forever with God, and saying yes to Jesus makes eternity your reality. Heaven is in your future.

But what about the time between here and heaven? How does God's plan include you? What's in store for all your tomorrows?

These verses in Jeremiah are another IFTTT statement by God. (And remember, he speaks only the truth.) He says, "I've got the very best in store for you. You couldn't ask for better!"

But in the next breath he tells us to do something: pray. In other words, God wants you to talk with him about your future.

As you learn to live out your new life in Christ this week, follow God's advice. Ask for a greater glimpse of who you are, and ask him what he has in store for your life. Because your identity and your future have a lot in common.

Question ?

What bigger or better things do you think God might have for you?

Challenge ❢

Ask your mentor about how God's plans have become a reality in their life.

°
(Thoughts)

Write down anything on your mind from day eight. Talk openly and honestly with your mentor about these questions and comments.

Practice Patience

The Lord is not slow in keeping his promise, as some understand slowness. Instead he is patient with you, not wanting anyone to perish, but everyone to come to repentance.

2 Peter 3:9 NIV

We live in a fast-paced world. Blazing Internet speeds. Instant downloads. Overnight delivery. Fast food. And cheetahs—they have to be on the list.

As life gets faster and faster, we get more and more impatient. We're an instant-gratification culture, which can be a problem when learning to wait on God. Because he isn't fast.

Oh, he can move quickly if he decides to do so. (Ever hear of the speed of light? Yeah. He created it.) But God takes his time with us so that his efforts can begin their good work in us. That's how he produces growth in our lives. Just like he waits for us to accept Jesus, we must also learn to practice patience. Transformation doesn't happen overnight.

Jesus is working in you to move you toward maturity. So trust him, and ask God to teach you how to wait. Don't worry and don't hurry. Hear his voice.

James was Jesus' half brother (they had the same mother, Mary, but James' father was a man named Joseph). Here's what he said about this issue:

"My fellow believers, when it seems as though you are facing nothing but difficulties see it as an invaluable opportunity to experience all the joy that you can! For you know that when your faith is tested it stirs up power within you to endure all things. And then as your endurance grows even stronger it will release perfection into every part of your being until there is nothing missing and nothing lacking" (James 1:2–4 TPT).

Don't listen to the voice of insecurity no matter how you feel or what others say. Remember your new identity. Think about what you're becoming. God waited for you, and he'll complete his work in you.

The world might be fast, but slow and steady finishes the race. Just take one day at a time.

Question ?

On a scale of 1 to 10, what's your patience level with yourself when you mess up? Do you think God leans more toward patience or frustration with you? What makes you think that?

Challenge !

Ask people who've been walking with Jesus about some time when they've experienced God's patience. Start by asking your mentor.

Thoughts

Write down anything on your mind from day nine. Talk openly and honestly with your mentor about these questions and comments.

Share Your Heart

And this is the confidence that we have toward him,
that if we ask anything according to his will he hears
us. And if we know that he hears us in whatever we
ask, we know that we have the requests that we
have asked of him.

1 John 5:14–15

Kindergartners have great imaginations. They
play dress-up and believe in fairy tales. They
dream about becoming astronauts and nurses,
presidents and pop stars. There's really no need to
teach five-year-olds to dream. It comes natural.

But then life happens. From adolescence to
adulthood, people tell us to color inside the lines.
Don't get your hopes up. Be realistic. Grow up.
Pretty soon we become apathetic about our desires.
We begin to suppress passion, emotion, and excite-
ment. After a while, many people give in. Some give
up and settle for average.

But God didn't make you for mediocrity. You've been invited into his story to continue Jesus' work. Here's what Jesus told his students:

"I tell you the truth, anyone who believes in me will do the same works I have done, and even greater works, because I am going to be with the Father. You can ask for anything in my name, and I will do it, so that the Son can bring glory to the Father" (John 14:12–13 NLT).

That's a promise. The goal is to pursue those things that Jesus wants you to dream about doing for him. As you listen to God and live out your identity in Christ, you'll understand more and more. You'll start to believe he can do the impossible through your life.

So start now. Share your heart. Tell God what you're passionate about. Express your thoughts, feelings, and ideas to him. He wants to hear from you. And don't worry. It's safe. Jesus will never dump cold water on your dreams.

Question ❓

What are your passions? What's something you love to do? What has bothered you for a long time that you want to do something about?

Challenge !

Dream! Think about how God might use your passions. Consider the idea that he put them inside you in the first place.

(Thoughts)

Write down anything on your mind from day ten. Talk openly and honestly with your mentor about these questions and comments.

Ask for Help

Your plans will fall apart right in front of you if you fail to get good advice. But if you first seek out multiple counselors, you'll watch your plans succeed.

Proverbs 15:22 TPT

When was the last time you needed help? And when was the last time you actually asked for it? Maybe it was from a family member or a friend. Or perhaps the problem wasn't personal at all. You might have just been stuck on an algebra assignment or a bit short on cash.

The depth of our difficulty dictates our willingness to ask for help. But some people refuse to rely on others—ever. No matter how difficult the homework or how desperate the situation, their pride prevents them from seeking support. They see it as a sign of weakness, so they try to handle it alone.

But God designed us to need each other. We discussed that even before we began day one. Our life experiences make us experts (or at least slightly less ignorant), so we must pass on the wisdom we've learned. We must never be too proud to raise our hand and ask for help. That's the real principle here: "Pride goes before destruction, and a haughty spirit before a fall" (Proverbs 16:18).

The partner you chose as a mentor has more practice with Jesus than you. They're not better, just more experienced (which means they've made more mistakes). But they probably do understand their identity in Christ to a deeper degree. So don't be too proud to depend on them, no matter the problem.

The simple practice of asking for help prevents pride and keeps you from becoming too big for your britches. We're never too old to not need guidance, so surround yourself with Christian companions to shoulder your problems with you. Then you'll never be alone.

Question ?

What stops you from going to other people for help?

Challenge ❗

List some of your fears about asking people for help.

⊶

(Thoughts)

Write down anything on your mind from day eleven. Talk openly and honestly with your mentor about these questions and comments.

Make a Bold Move

> And Peter answered him, "Lord, if it is you, command me to come to you on the water." He said, "Come." So Peter got out of the boat and walked on the water and came to Jesus.
>
> *Matthew 14:28–29*

World changers risk failure. They consider the costs and make calculated decisions. But at some point they must pull the trigger and take action. Nothing changes if nothing changes. And nothing good comes from being complacent.

Sometimes risk takers jump off cliffs, then figure out how to fly as they're falling. You dove into the deep end of the Jesus pool before you knew how to swim, so your crazy move puts you in really good company.

Peter did the same thing. He took a chance and followed Jesus, and over time he learned to recognize his teacher's voice. So when Peter heard his teacher say, "Come," he didn't hesitate to jump out of the boat. He knew Jesus wouldn't let him down—or let him drown.

Too many people never put their faith into action. They either let fear stop them or they look for the approval of others. Both are dream killers.

God didn't invite you to accept Jesus just to change you internally. He cast you in his story to be a catalyst for world change externally too. You're a playmaker with a purpose, but let's get something straight: Your strength comes from Christ—in you. And the passions he wired within you must be used to accomplish his plan.

For eleven days, you've been patient to practice treading water. But it's time to make a bold move and act on what Jesus has been revealing. Now bold moves don't always mean big moves. Think about what you've been learning about your identity. Consider leaving your comfort zone, and ask Jesus to show you a small but significant step you can take today.

Question ?

What is the hardest thing you imagine God might ask you to do?

Challenge ❗

Ask God to give you the courage to trust him to do hard things.

°
○

(Thoughts)

Write down anything on your mind from day twelve. Talk openly and honestly with your mentor about these questions and comments.

Learn from Your Mistakes

But when he saw the wind, he was afraid, and beginning to sink he cried out, "Lord, save me." Jesus immediately reached out his hand and took hold of him, saying to him, "O you of little faith, why did you doubt?"

Matthew 14:30–31

Your best teacher is your last mistake."

"A mistake is only a mistake if you don't learn anything from it."

"If you're not making mistakes, then you're not doing anything."

A quick Internet search will reveal thousands of quotes like these. Sometimes the ideas are inspiring. And other times they're just irritating. We can't always rely on clever clichés to motivate us at those moments of failure. Learning the hard way hurts. But it is—or needs to be—a part of life.

Your new identity in Christ doesn't create immunity from making mistakes. God doesn't promise that we won't mess up as we follow Jesus. Actually, it's pretty much a guarantee that we will. So the best way to deal with the inevitable is to expect it, admit it, and learn from it. (By the way, did you notice how this is another way to help prevent pride?)

Peter stepped out of the boat. That was bold. But then he felt the pressure. He got worried about the waves, and about as quickly as he was walking on water, he found himself swallowing water. Why? Well, he blinked.

Peter took his eyes off Jesus, and he began to sink. And Peter was a big deal! If it could happen to him, it can happen to the best of us. So don't let people beat you up for blowing it while trying to take a risk for Jesus.

You're going to fall down from time to time. When you do, follow Peter's example. Call out to Jesus. He'll pick you up, put you back in the boat, and prepare you for your next bold move. In Jesus, you can learn from your mistakes.

Question ?

What mistakes have you made in your life that were painful?

Challenge !

Take a few minutes to write down the mistakes you made and the lessons you learned from them.

Thoughts

Write down anything on your mind from day thirteen. Talk openly and honestly with your mentor about these questions and comments.

Day 14

Rest and Repeat

For I can do everything through Christ, who gives me strength.

Philippians 4:13 NLT

Have you ever been involved in an activity that required you to give everything you had—110 percent—and then some? Maybe it was a championship game that took every ounce of energy you could find. Perhaps it was finishing a difficult project, cramming for an exam, or completing a course.

Life can be physically and emotionally draining, especially when you're in over your head and you can't touch the bottom. But there's good news: You've made it through another seven days of intense initiation. Today marks the end of two weeks of deep-water training. You've earned another real rest, so it's time for some recovery and reflection.

Learning to live out your new identity in Christ can be hard work. For that reason, today is a review, not a task or a test. If you're feeling weary or overwhelmed, don't worry. Remember where your strength comes from.

When you said yes to following Jesus, he took up residence in your heart. There's nothing he can't do through you. Here's a great verse to encourage you:

"We all experience times of testing, which is normal for every human being. But God will be faithful to you. He will screen and filter the severity, nature, and timing of every test or trial you face so that you can bear it. And each test is an opportunity to trust him more, for along with every trial God has provided for you a way of escape that will bring you out of it victoriously" (1 Corinthians 10:13 TPT).

Choosing to follow Jesus can be challenging. You might have already encountered some resistance. But there's no need to view your opposition as obstacles. They're just opportunities for you to rest and repeat everything you've learned as you rely on Jesus every day.

Question ❓

When have you considered giving up because something was just too hard to finish?

Challenge 🕯

If there are things you've quit in the past that need to be completed, make a plan go back and get them done.

(Thoughts)

Write down anything on your mind from day fourteen. Talk openly and honestly with your mentor about these questions and comments.

Week 3

VOICE

Britain's *Got Talent* is a British talent show that has swept the globe. The program originally aired in 2005, and so far has spawned spin-offs in fifty-eight nations. Countless contestants have lined up for a chance in the spotlight. From singers to sword swallowers, dancers to daredevils, there's no shortage of people looking for a shot to show off.

In addition to offering a few minutes of fame, *BGT* also promises a substantial cash prize for the winner. But is fame or money the real reason participants make themselves vulnerable to viewers? Or is there something more substantial motivating them to risk failure and face humiliation in front of millions of people?

Let's go with the latter because down deep we all want to matter, to have a voice, and to feel valued.

Social media has changed the game in this area. It lets us share our passions or positions immediately. People can post their point of view from just about anywhere. Anytime. About anything. We even carry a digital platform for being heard in the palm of our hand.

Yet having an audience at your fingertips must be about more than just having a chance to share your opinion. There may be people who will always like your posts, but that doesn't mean they value your voice or hear your heart.

Finding your voice in God's story is this week's focus. Take note though: having a voice is about more than just being able to say something—it's about having something to say.

Since the first day of *Begin21*, you've been cultivating your relationship with Jesus. You've put practices in place to nurture your need to know God. Last week, we focused on living out your newly found identity, which comes from a sense of belonging in Jesus. You may have noticed that we followed a formula to get to this point in the process:

Relationship + Identity = Voice.

Here's a better breakdown of the recipe: Your relationship with God gives you identity, your identity in Christ gives you value, and your value gives you a voice. And you have something to say!

God invited you into his story to tell others about his plan for the world and his purpose for their lives. But you might be thinking, *I'm not prepared to do that. How would I express my voice in a way that others will want to listen?* Simple. Share your story, and show how your life has changed since Jesus Christ became your hero (see day five).

While you're gearing up and getting ready to use the voice God has given you, keep following the formula: Relationship + Identity = Voice. Your first fourteen steps have prepared you for the next seven. There'll never be a shortage of opportunities for you to share God's story and showcase Jesus. The world is your stage—your space in the spotlight.

You have a song to sing and people are listening, so find your voice and use it.

Day 15

Put Others First

Is there any encouragement from belonging to Christ? Any comfort from his love? Any fellowship together in the Spirit? Are your hearts tender and compassionate? Then make me truly happy by agreeing wholeheartedly with each other, loving one another, and working together with one mind and purpose. Don't be selfish; don't try to impress others. Be humble, thinking of others as better than yourselves.

Philippians 2:1–3 NLT

Do you know someone who has ever trained for a competition of any kind with the goal of coming in last? Of course not. That wouldn't make any sense at all. We like to be number one.

So we work hard. We practice and we sacrifice all for the purpose of taking first place. We're wired to win.

But can you be the best and be last at the same

time? Is that even possible? The answer is ... drum roll, please ... yes! Definitely. Not only is it possible, but it's also today's principle. We're going to take this point of view directly from Jesus' playbook. It's called *I'm Third*, and here's what it means: Jesus comes first. Others come second. We take last place.

He explains it to his students this way: "It shall not be so among you. But whoever would be great among you must be your servant, and whoever would be first among you must be your slave, even as the Son of Man came not to be served but to serve, and to give his life as a ransom for many" (Matthew 20:26–28).

You're in God's story because Jesus *chose to lose*. He gave his life on a cross so you could have a full and lasting life. He put you first. He let you win. That's how the love of God works.

When we help others get ahead, they notice. People feel loved because putting others ahead of ourselves is so different from the ways of the world. Stepping aside makes you stand out and gives your voice value. So put others first today. Practice being third.

You'll earn the right to be heard.

Question ?

Can you remember a time when someone went out of their way to help you with a problem? How did it make you feel? How does going out of your way to put someone else first make you feel about yourself?

Challenge !

Think about the people you pass every day. Imagine slowing down enough to notice what's going on in their lives. Put your needs last today to help at least one person.

Thoughts

Write down anything on your mind from day fifteen. Talk openly and honestly with your mentor about these questions and comments.

Start Listening

My dear brothers and sisters, take note of this:
Everyone should be quick to listen, slow to speak
and slow to become angry.

James 1:19 NIV

More than likely, you have two ears on your head. One might be slightly lower or larger than the other, but at least your sunglasses sit fairly straight.

God gave us ears for more than balancing sunglasses and piercing. Their primary purpose is to help us hear (which is often considered the most important sense that humans have). If it weren't for our ears, we'd miss the sounds of our surroundings: gentle blowing breezes, laughter, music, and voices that beg for our attention. Hearing is also vital to survival because it alerts us and allows us to get out of harm's way.

Apart from a segment of our society that lives with deafness, most people can hear just fine. And for those with a perfectly good sense of hearing, there's no excuse for not listening. It's rude—and it's painful for others. Poor listening diminishes other people's dignity while good listening lets them know they matter.

If you want others to hear your voice, you don't have to shout. There's no need to use a megaphone or talk over a crowd. You just have to eavesdrop on the echoes of life. If you learn to listen, others will be quicker to listen to you.

Here are a few quick tips and techniques to help you become a better listener:

1. Make eye contact: this is about them.
2. Stop talking: this isn't about you.
3. Hear ideas: this is about their thoughts.
4. Ask questions: this isn't about your answers

When listening becomes a lifestyle, people will want to hear what you have to say. The best way to share your story is to start by shutting your mouth. Start listening.

Question ❓

When was the last time you felt like someone really took the time to listen to you? How often do you refrain from giving your opinion so you can listen to the ideas of others?

Challenge ❗

Think about a person who is going through a difficult time right now. Go out of your way to ask them about their situation. You might just hear their pain and help protect them from harm.

⸖ (Thoughts)

Write down anything on your mind from day sixteen. Talk openly and honestly with your mentor about these questions and comments.

Day 17

Don't Pretend

If anyone imagines that he knows something, he does not yet know as he ought to know. But if anyone loves God, he is known by God.

1 Corinthians 8:2–3

Have you ever met a know-it-all? You know, the person with a lot of head knowledge who loves to correct you and share what they know.

You: Yesterday was the hottest day of the summer.

Know-It-All: Actually, the hottest day of the summer this year was August fourth.

You: Okay. Whatever. Anyway, it was really hot, so I put on SPF 75 sunscreen before I mowed the yard.

Know-It-All: You know there's no point in applying an SPF over 50, right?

There's one word for that kind of dialogue:

77

annoying. Nobody likes a know-it-all. But the world is full of these people who think they have all the answers. Don't be that person.

Now is an important time in your relationship with Jesus to admit that you're a newbie—that there's a lot you don't know yet. But you will. In time, you'll master the deep end of the pool and be ready to instruct others. Until then—and even after then—your simple story speaks volumes.

A teacher named Paul said it this way in the Bible: "And so it was with me, brothers and sisters. When I came to you, I did not come with eloquence or human wisdom as I proclaimed to you the testimony about God. For I resolved to know nothing while I was with you except Jesus Christ and him crucified" (1 Corinthians 2:1–2 NIV).

As people begin to listen to your voice, don't pretend you have all of God or all of life figured out. Be humble. Just tell them what you know about Jesus so far, and confess that you still have an awful lot to learn.

Question ?

What's the first word that comes to your mind when you think of a person who always has to be right about everything? Why do you think they feel the need to correct others?

Challenge)

Be aware of your words today to make sure you don't come across as a know-it-all. It's as easy as asking more questions and giving fewer answers.

°
o
(Thoughts)

Write down anything on your mind from day seventeen. Talk openly and honestly with your mentor about these questions and comments.

Day 18

Take Action

What good is it, my brothers, if someone says he has faith but does not have works? Can that faith save him?

James 2:14

If You See Something, Say Something™ is a public awareness campaign by the United States Department of Homeland Security. It was created to urge people to report suspicious activity of terrorism and terrorism-related crime to law enforcement.

The need for such a campaign in the United States is unfortunate, and America is certainly not the only nation at great risk. The world is a perilous place and it's growing more and more dangerous every day.

Was this part of God's original wish for our world? Not at all. Humankind basically blew it from the very beginning. Sin entered the earth when Adam and Eve decided to do things their way and plunged the planet into a tailspin. This created separation between God and his creation.

This is the exact reason God sent Jesus. He came to bring the world back to God—to save it. That's why we call him our Savior. After his death and resurrection, he ascended into heaven, but someday he'll return. The good news is that when he does, the world will be restored back to the way God first intended.

So what do we do until then? Sit around and wait? No. We use our voice to tell God's story of Jesus. That's a good start. But as everyone knows, talk alone is cheap.

Our planet will be perfect again when Christ comes back. In the meantime, we must fight injustice in Jesus' name. Just as Jesus stood up and stretched out his arms for the broken, we must do the same. We must reach out to the marginalized, lift up those who have been oppressed, and put our faith to work.

So here's our public awareness campaign: *If You See Something, Do Something—Take Action.*

Question ❓

What new needs have you noticed since you started following Jesus? What have you done with your time to offer a hand or make a difference for those issues?

Challenge ❗

Choose a cause that breaks your heart today and determine to do something about it. Go to wavesinaction.com right now to learn how to start a WAVES group of your own.

Thoughts

Write down anything on your mind from day eighteen. Talk openly and honestly with your mentor about these questions and comments.

Speak Reality

Jesus said to him, "I am the way, and the truth, and the life. No one comes to the Father except through me. If you had known me, you would have known my Father also. From now on you do know him and have seen him."

John 14:6–7

Wake up and smell the coffee!"

"Pull your head out of the sand!"

"Come back down to earth!"

These expressions aren't compliments. We use them when someone refuses to face the facts or when they're living in denial. Usually we say them out of frustration or irritation because we care for the person. We just wish they'd accept reality.

When life gets too hard to handle, people look for a way out of their mess. They seek a source of recovery. Some run. And some go to rehab.

You turned to Jesus.

You heard God's voice, made a choice, and took the unpopular path. Your choice resulted from a belief that Jesus is the way forward—that he is the only road that leads to a full and lasting life.

So many people live in a false reality. They lie to themselves to create the world they want. Instead of facing the facts, they create their own truth. And they pay a high price for their self-deception: "Before every person there is a path that seems like the right one to take, but it leads them straight to hell!" (Proverbs 16:25 TPT).

We live in a world of lies that lead to devastation. Destruction. Death. But you now know the difference is named Jesus, so you must use your voice to help others wake up and smell the coffee.

There's only one way to God, no matter what skeptics may say. Even so, don't be frustrated with people. Be patient, and continue to humbly speak reality.

Question ❓

How do you feel about the idea of relative truth *that basically says,* If you believe it, it's true for you; if I don't believe it, it's not true for me? *How will you respond to*

*that concept now that Jesus is your reality—that he is
the truth?*

Challenge ❗

*You will be asked to back up what you believe about
Jesus. Don't check your brain at the door. Consider
how you can learn to defend your faith.*

Thoughts

*Write down anything on your mind from day nineteen.
Talk openly and honestly with your mentor about these
questions and comments.*

Spread Hope

Blessed be the God and Father of our Lord Jesus Christ! According to his great mercy, he has caused us to be born again to a living hope through the resurrection of Jesus Christ from the dead, to an inheritance that is imperishable, undefiled, and unfading, kept in heaven for you, who by God's power are being guarded through faith for a salvation ready to be revealed in the last time.

1 Peter 1:3–5

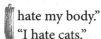 hate my body."

"I hate cats."

"I hate school."

"I hate politics."

"I hate war."

"I hate you."

We use the word *hate* way too easily. How sad we have become because of this word, *hate*. Hate will never heal. Hate only leads to more hurt. If we want to join God in his work, expressions of hate must be replaced with expressions of hope. *Hope* is a better word for us than *hate*.

When we dream of better days and brighter futures, we don't think of adding more pain, suffering, and selfishness to the world. Those aren't attributes of optimism. They're aspects of everything that is wrong around us, and people aren't seeking more sorrow.

Anyone can tear down. That doesn't take special powers. It's easy to criticize and condemn. But building up instead of belittling? That requires real effort.

Jesus is alive, and he's working in you and through you to transform your world. The forgiveness, confidence, and peace you have in him must be shared. God's message to the world isn't worry or fear, doom or gloom. Jesus died to remove darkness. He defeated death to give us life. And he'll return to restore the planet. Everything will be made new. No more pain. No more sorrow. Good-bye tears. Adios disease. Arrivederci death.

But hope isn't just a future event. It's a daily demonstration of God's love flowing through you now. So don't just wait for the day when Jesus comes back to correct the world's wrongs. Be pro-active. Take a stand. Be a light. And in everything you do, spread hope!

Question ❓

Why is it easier for people to be pessimistic and focus on the negative? Why do you think there's a growing sense of hopelessness throughout the world?

Challenge ❗

Use your voice today to be a messenger of hope. Think of a topic you can speak to with positive words that offer practical solutions. Share that hope with someone.

Thoughts

Write down anything on your mind from day twenty. Talk openly and honestly with your mentor about these questions and comments.

Day 21

Give God Credit

The end of all things is at hand; therefore be self-controlled and sober-minded for the sake of your prayers. Above all, keep loving one another earnestly, since love covers a multitude of sins. Show hospitality to one another without grumbling. As each has received a gift, use it to serve one another, as good stewards of God's varied grace: whoever speaks, as one who speaks oracles of God; whoever serves, as one who serves by the strength that God supplies—in order that in everything God may be glorified through Jesus Christ. To him belong glory and dominion forever and ever. Amen.

1 Peter 4:7–11

Me, *myself*, and *I*. These are the most popular pronouns in our vocabulary. We love to talk about ourselves and post our own praises. We want to claim responsibility for all that is good in the world.

People produce good things, right? Sure they do. So it only seems reasonable to receive recognition for our efforts, right? Yes. But for the sake of argument, let's put our human nature on hold for a moment and recall where this all-that-is-good idea got its start: "God saw all that he had made, and it was very good" (Genesis 1:31 NIV).

Life began with God, and all that he created was good. Then sin entered the picture and we were separated from perfection. But God gave us a way back to him by giving us Jesus. We did nothing. He did it all.

Your new life in Christ comes from him. It also belongs to him. Jesus is your reality. He's your hope. He handpicked you. On purpose. For his purposes. And you can't ever forget that he rescued you.

He, *him*, and *his*. These are now the most important pronouns you possess. The world is going to ask, "What happened to you? What makes you different? Why are you living this way?" When they do, pause to remember. Then give God credit.

Question ❓

When was the last time you received credit for something you did? Think about how being praised for your

*efforts made you feel. If you can't recall ever getting rec-
ognition, think about how that makes you feel.*

Challenge !

*Make a list of everything God has done for you in the
last twenty-one days. Share that list with someone who
might be ready to listen to your story and hear about
Jesus.*

Thoughts

*Write down anything on your mind from day twenty-one.
Talk openly and honestly with your mentor about these
questions and comments.*

Your Next Steps

The last twenty-one days have been a crash course in following Jesus Christ. You've accomplished a lot in such a short time, so be pleased with your progress.

The core lessons of the Christian life are critical. So that's what we covered in *Begin21*. We focused on the fundamentals. Why? Because you can always return to the basics. These principles will never fail if you practice them.

But there's more for you to learn, and it only gets better and better. Instead of just barely keeping your head above water, you'll be doing the back-stroke. Others will be learning from your life. Your craving for Jesus will be contagious.

This is a good place to remind you that following Jesus won't always be easy. We mentioned that in the introduction. There's evil in the world, and we have a spiritual enemy that wants you to fail: "Be alert and of sober mind. Your enemy the devil prowls around like a roaring lion looking for someone to devour. Resist him, standing firm in the faith, because you know that the family of believers throughout the world is undergoing the same kind of suffering" (1 Peter 5:8–9 NIV).

If following Jesus ever feels like a fight, it's because you're in a dangerous battle with the devil. He's a villain, but his attacks are in vain. You are already victorious. Jesus has already won the war no matter what the world wants you to believe: "Little children, you are from God and have overcome them, for he who is in you is greater than he who is in the world" (1 John 4:4).

Be confident. Be courageous. The same power that raised Jesus from the dead lives in you. He is your strength, and he'll never abandon you. Jesus assured us, "I have said these things to you, that in me you may have peace. In the world you will have tribulation. But take heart; I have overcome the world" (John 16:33).

Remember everything you've learned in the last three weeks. Stay connected to your mentor and your new Christian companions. Rinse. Lather. And repeat.

Build your relationship with Jesus. Live out your new identity. Use the voice God has given you to tell your story. And then help others accept God's invitation.

✳✳✳

Ready to go deeper?
For more resources to build your relationship
with Jesus, go to **EndeavorResources.org**.

About the Author

Timothy Eldred has been in youth ministry for over twenty-five years. His role as lead pastor of New Beginnings is just a disguise; he's a youth worker at heart. Since 2005, he's also served as president of Endeavor Ministries, which has trained millions of young leaders globally since 1881. Each year, Tim travels extensively, speaking and consulting on the biblical model of youth in ministry. His Grow21 discipleship series books have been used by five hundred thousand teens worldwide.

Currently, Tim is completing his PhD with Trinity Theological Seminary.

Above all else, Tim's most important role takes place in Edmore, Michigan, where he and his wife of twenty-six years, Cindy, have raised their two sons to follow Jesus Christ.

Find Tim online at TimothyEldred.com
on Facebook at Facebook.com/timothyeldred
or on Twitter @timothyeldred